The 4 Cornerstones Of Your Success

"Building A Life Beyond Your Imagination"

ISBN 978-0-9905111-0-6 paperback

ISBN 978-0-9905111-1-3 e-book

Author: Dre Parker

Design: Lavish Lyfe Design

WWW.VISUALIZEDWEALTH.COM

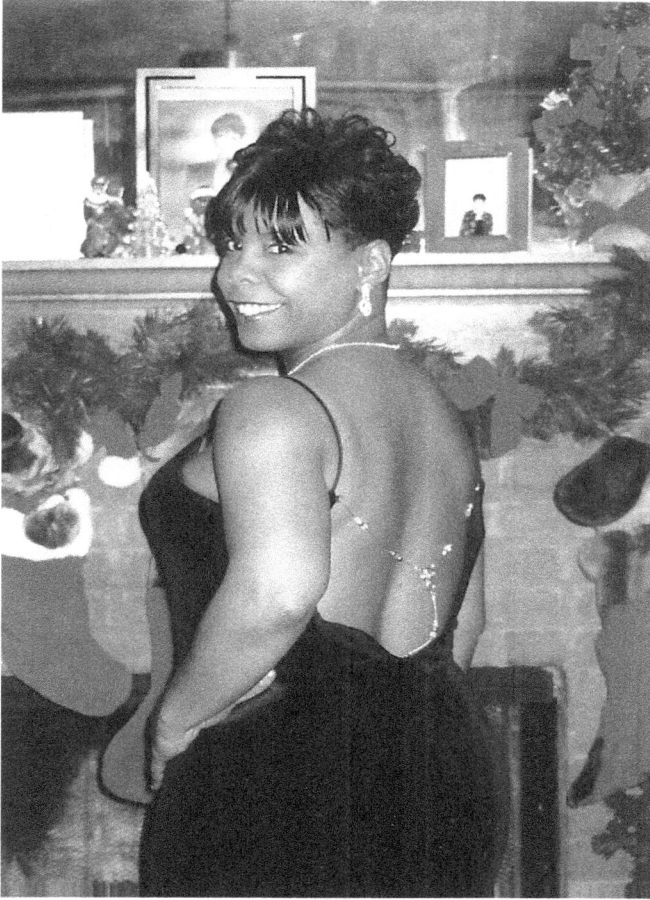

In Loving Memory Of
Pamela Joi Jones Ashbourne

August 24, 1962 – May 4, 2014

DEDICATION

I dedicate this book to all of humanity. It is a piece of me. It's for those who know me and those that do not know me. I have had the privilege to change my life through these four cornerstones, and now I am in the field of changing other people's lives with them. I believe it is a collaborative effort on all of our parts to make things better.

A special dedication goes to my Aunt Pam who recently passed away from lung cancer. She was like a mother to me. She has cared for and loved our family beyond imagination. She was the epitome of a giving person. She has further confirmed to me the powers of these cornerstones in our lives. This is also dedicated in memory of my loving grandmothers, Thelma L. Holley and Jennie Hill. They were the examples of strong women in my life.

I will be donating $1 from each book sold to help with the fight against lung cancer in memory of Pamela Joi Jones-Ashbourne. Carolyn "Dinkey" Lockhart, and Thelma Holley.   Lung cancer has claimed more lives than breast, prostate, colon, liver, kidney, and melanoma cancers combined! Let's help those who are still fighting this horrible disease.

ACKNOWLEDGEMENTS

First and foremost, I would like to thank God for all that I am and all that I will be. Throughout life, we grab hold to a belief system that allows us to achieve amazing things while we are here. I attribute all of my accomplishments seen and unseen to the Source of it all.

I would like to thank my mother, Eva L. Shorter, for instilling in me some great values and teaching me the meaning of love and hard work. I would like to thank my father, Donald Parker, as well. I would like to thank all of my mentors throughout my life. There are too many to mention, but the gratitude goes to each and every one of you. I would like to thank all my friends who truly believe in me and have pushed me to greatness.

My family is a key factor in my life. I thank them for all of the love and support in all of my endeavors. I want to thank my children, Kedar Mikel Parker, Imani J'nae Parker, and Micah Nasir Parker, for being a big part of my "why" in life. I have to send a special thanks to my beautiful wife of 13 years, LaShonda Parker, for sticking with me throughout the years. You are truly a blessing, and I thank you so much for staying by my side and experiencing this thing we call "life" together.

CONTENTS

Forward

As far as I could remember, I have been fascinated with success. There are many definitions of what "success" means to different people. One thing I tell people to realize is that if you are determining your success based upon material things, then you are in for many disappointments throughout life.

Success has to be thought of first as an idea. Once you achieve or accomplish that idea, then you are successful. As anything else in life, there are levels to success. Those levels are determined by the parameters that one sets.

The purpose of this book is to give you the four most important areas that you need to build to have a completely successful life. The 4 Cornerstones To Your Success was written not just to inform you of what you need, but also to inspire you and give you the tools to accomplish those things that you want out of life.

My company has a program called Visualized Wealth 360. It represents your completion to your success. 360 degrees is always looked at as a circle. Today, I want you to look at it as a square. "Why the square," you may ask? Well, in math both of those shapes equal 360 degrees. We must learn how to take what the infinite mind has given us and learn how to confine it to our understanding. That's the reason for the square. The circle is infinite and the square is finite. The four areas I believe that give you that completion would be faith, family, fitness, and finance. I will touch on each of these areas as we progress into this book.

I want you to understand what I mean by "wealth". Let's look at the etymology of the word wealth. Wealth (n.) mid-13c., "happiness," also "prosperity in abundance of possessions or riches," from Middle English *wele* "well-being". So, you see it's not all about material possessions.

The reason the word, "visualized" is used in the past tense is because once you get a vision of it, your next step is to make it real. From the present on, you can only move forward into the future, which leaves that moment in the past. I want you to see it as if it has already happened.

I am absolutely sure that once you master these four areas of your life, you will have found the magic potion that all are searching for. You see, it's not about being balanced; it's about being whole. We work on different areas of our lives at different times. This is not an easy task that you will complete after one reading. This book is to only give you the blueprint and the tools to build a great life. You still remain the architect and the builder.

Nowadays, most people are looking for quick solutions to life's problems.

Understand that life moves on a continuum. You will get to different areas of your life when it is the right time. The only way to speed up the process is to first become aware of the process and then work on it diligently.

Let's dive into the first cornerstone of our journey so we can live the successful life we all want and dream of.

"Now faith is the substance of things hoped for, the evidence of things not seen"
Hebrews 11:1

ONE

Faith

"Faith is taking the first step even when you don't see the whole staircase"- Martin Luther King, Jr.

Many of us want to see the complete path to our success not realizing that it doesn't exist yet. You may say, "Before I make a decision, I need to see step by step how it's going to work." Well, if seeing is believing, then you are not much of a believer. Then there are those who say, "I will believe it when I see it." No, you see it when you believe it. You have to have faith and huge vision first.

The thing I love most about this cornerstone is that you can have any type of religious or even scientific background, but you still need this key element. You see, "faith" leads to "facts". No one escapes this element. Whether you have an abundance of it or a lack there of, your world is shaped around this. The more faith you have, the more substantial your life becomes.

Going back 10 years ago, I will never forget my wife walking into our bedroom saying to me, "Honey I want to have another baby and I want to go to nursing school." I looked at her as if she were crazy. The reason? At that time we weren't making a lot of money, and we already had two kids. I was working a job I couldn't stand, and I was also working on my music career as a producer and songwriter. Anyone who knows anything about the music business knows it's one of the most difficult industries to break into.

So, there we were - financially struggling. She wasn't happy on her job so she made the decision to go back to school.

She said, "I will continue working while I take my prerequisites, but I will be in the accelerated nursing program; so, I will have to quit working."

"What?!" I replied. "How is that going to work?"

"I don't know," she said, "but we will figure it out."

So, after our son was born, my wife continued to work while taking her prerequisites. I was at my wits end with my job. I knew that once she stopped working, it would be impossible to leave. An opportunity presented itself to work for a gentleman who owned a painting company. I decided to jump on board. I didn't have much of a plan, but my faith was strong in knowing it would all work out.

Well, as life would have it, working for this gentleman didn't pan out like I expected. Let's just say after one month of work, I never got a paycheck. I had to make a decision quickly on what to do.

Never letting go of my faith, I continued to explore other options as an entrepreneur. One month later, I ended up being in the right place at the right time. I landed the opportunity to take over my uncle's small landscaping company.

I was pulling in good money, which really helped, but then the next obstacle occurred. My wife got accepted into the accelerated nursing program at Georgia State University, which meant that once she started she wouldn't be working for the next two years. Although making good money with my small landscaping company, I knew it wouldn't be enough financially to take care of all the household expenses. After calculating the mortgage, childcare, recurring bills, and the most important, food, we would end up being in the negative each month.

I said frantically to my wife, "There is no way we can make this happen mathematically!"

She gave me a look and said, "There is no way I can work and do the accelerated program at the same time!"

So, here we are again testing good old faith.

I looked at her and said, "Well, I guess we will have to make it work then."

Needless to say, two years later, after a lot of financial bumps and bruises, we made it out alive. Looking back, I must say that was one of the best decisions we've made for our family. Now, I can fully concentrate on my businesses while she has the career she dreamed about.

Most people try to see the whole stairway before they take the first step. Our story is a prime example of not even seeing the path, but seeing the end destination. You see, we have to create our own path to reach our destination. Many of us are looking for the navigation system of faith that gives us an overview of our journey. Unfortunately, it doesn't exist. If you were to type in the address to success, the route of your destination would look something like this:

Travel 2 miles until you come to a complete stop because of the wall in front of you. Now, climb the wall because you can't go left or right. Once over the wall, continue on your journey for another 5 miles until you get to a marsh. Go through the marsh, but be careful of the dangers that exist while traveling through it. Once through the marsh, continue on through uncharted territory for an unknown amount of time until you get to a mountain. Once you climb over the mountain, your destination will be 2 miles down on the left. However, beware because just a few feet before you reach your destination, your GPS will reboot because there is no satellite signal.

You see, in that example, some people will continue forward and some people will just stop and turnaround. Many of us are so close to what we want;

however, because faith disappeared, we no longer move forward.

Faith is the element that you will need throughout all of your travels in this life. While obtaining knowledge and wisdom on any subject, it will start with the belief that, I *can do this.* You see, that's why I say faith leads to facts. Faith in the science world is nothing more than a belief in a hypothesis (educated guess). It starts off as a belief that it can happen, but once tried and tested, it becomes "real". The problem most people have is that they let their physical eyes guide and direct them. If you go by what you see physically, or should I say *sight* instead of *vision*, then you limit your possibilities.

What does it profit, my brethren, if someone says he has faith but does not have works? Can faith save him"? –James 2:14

Faith without works is definitely dead. Your success will not happen if you don't become a part of it. You have to work for it, period. In the grand design of things, that's how it works. It would be useless to have some great idea that never manifests because you decided to just have faith in it.

I have spent the earlier part of my life around people with great ideas. Unfortunately, I realized most of those people where dreamers, and not doers. Now, there is nothing wrong with being a dreamer. I must say I am a dreamer myself. The only difference in making your dream a reality is the work you put into it. You see, anyone can have a dream but it takes a special person to work that dream and see it through.

Even if it seems "unrealistic" and "crazy" to those who don't understand it, the faith you have in an idea can change the course of the world. Look at the Wright brothers, for instance. The two American brothers were inventors and aviation pioneers who were credited for building the world's first successful airplane. Although they were not the first to build and fly experimental aircrafts, their persistency and faith to make it better led them to become the fathers of modern aviation.

There are several acronyms for the word faith; however, I came up with one that I think really signifies what needs to happen. Faith = **F**ocus **A**ll **I**n **T**hrough **H**ope. You see, faith is something that's not tangible. So, here is where *focusing all in through hope* comes in. Focusing brings about a concentrated awareness of a thing. The true law of attraction comes from this. What you focus on, you will attract to you or see more of.

For instance if you are looking for a new house, all of a sudden you will start to notice more "For Sale" signs while you are traveling throughout your city or town. Does that mean they weren't there before? No, it doesn't. It only means your focus has changed and now you are attracting that which you are seeking.

Your focus has to be *all in* to make faith so thick and "real" that you will need a knife to cut through it.

Focusing all in through hope. Well, you see faith and hope go hand in hand. Your complete focus on faith will lead you through hope. Hope is defined as *something that is desired or expected*. When you work your faith, you will go through hope and create all you desire. This process makes it "real". That's why I use the term "through hope." When you go through something, you are traveling from the point at which you started until you get to the end. This end will be a new time reference and a new place in your life. So, when you are struggling or going through a difficult time in your life, always remember, "This too shall pass". There are no exceptions.

"Fear knocked at the door. Faith opened the door and there was no one there." Anonymous

This quote is the epitome of the resilience of faith! In order for success to come to you, there is a battle that has to be fought. All of us have to go through this fight. Fear and faith can be compared to a boxing match. However, both opponents are evenly matched. Fear is in one corner towering 7 feet tall weighing a sleek 250 lbs, while faith is in the other corner with the same credentials. The only way either one of them can win is by focusing. *You* have to be the deciding factor. It has to be a complete decision on your part in order for either one to win. Which do you choose?

And he said unto them, Why are ye fearful, O ye of little faith? -Matthew 8:26, King James Bible.

Most of us at some point become afraid to take action because of the fear of failure. The reason faith is the first cornerstone is because without it anything you attempt to do will end up in automatic failure. You know the old saying, *"You have*

15

to believe to achieve." There is truth to that. Understand this; most people don't even start because they have allowed fear to resonate in their spirit. There is greatness in the human spirit. The degrees of infinite potential can't be comprehended by limited minds. There are no limited people, just limited minds.

Just like the body needs to be exercised in order to achieve greater power, strength, and endurance so does your faith. One of the greatest solutions to keeping strong faith is to keep a positive attitude. Most people will get defensive and say, "I do have a positive attitude!" I want you to really analyze your thoughts for a moment. You see, it's really circumstantial. Take this scenario for example:

Imagine you are on your job. Now this isn't particularly the job of your dreams; however, there are days when you enjoy it. Let's say you work with a group of people and most of them complain daily. The company just implemented a new system that you don't particularly care for. You happened to be amongst the co-workers who are complaining when your boss comes in and says, "John, I need you and the team to transfer all data from the old system to the new system by Friday."(It's Monday so you only have 5 days to do so.)

In your mind you say, "There is no way we can do all of that by Friday and still continue with everyday tasks!"

So of course the team shares in your frustrations, which is warranted. You say to yourself, "This is last minute planning! Management hasn't a clue on how to run things around here!"

Now, you have spawned a series of negative thoughts from, *"there's no way"* to *"management is incompetent"*. Here's the problem. You don't plan on quitting your job any time soon; so, you really need to make this happen.

In scenarios like this, you must learn how to be positive. Although the first thought that crossed your mind may have been negative, always remember, what you focus on is what you will bring about. Instead of joining the collective thoughts of negativity, you must conclude in your mind that this task must be done and immediately stop with the complaints. Remember, drawn out complaints do nothing but reinforce negativity and create non-productive results. Instead, put in your mind the positives of completing the task and being the best you can be in all situations. Creating that type of mindset along with the right work ethic will put everything in your favor.

There will always be circumstances that interfere with the goals you would like to achieve. That's just the way it is. The only thing that must change is **YOU**. Your outlook has to be redefined and reshaped.

The reason negativity prevails in the media is because our collective minds naturally latch on to it. The power of focus can change that, but it starts within our own world. The inner world we create will determine the outer world we see.

How do we keep a positive attitude most of the time, you ask? It's simple, but not easy. Become aware of your thoughts, your words, and your surroundings. I have worked around negative people before but I've learned the trick is not to transfer their energy onto myself. How do you do that? Remember, we talked about attraction? Remember, we talked about focus? Right, that's it! First, I had to change internally with my own thoughts and words. Then eventually, my surroundings changed. There is a difference between a negative person and a person being negative. I have eliminated all negative people out of my life because they cannot exist in a positive space and vice versa.

You want to exercise your mind by focusing on positive thoughts and training it to visualize positive imagery. Having faith gives you the feeling of confidence and conviction. You cannot have faith if you are in a state of being fearful. Fear robs you of your faith! Conquer the fear and allow faith to grow; then watch more success happen in your life.

TWO

Family

"A happy family is but an earlier heaven". - George Bernard Shaw

The second cornerstone to your success is family. Although some may disagree with this, I believe family is essential to your success. By family, I don't always mean your immediate bloodline. You see, some people have the misconception that success can happen without the help of anyone else. On the contrary, no one becomes successful alone. Even with something as powerful as intrinsic motivation and determination, nothing happens alone. For example, as great and talented as Michael Jordan was, he still had a coach and a mentor.

There is a collaborative effort by the universe to bring success to you, but it is shared collectively. When playing for the Chicago Bulls was Michael Jordan the only winner of the championship games? No, everyone on the team won. The city of Chicago won, along with all of the fans across the world. Everyone shares in the success of the win.

Family values transcend your bloodline because it's something that is innate in human beings. People are strongly motivated to have relationships. There is a basic psychological need to feel closely connected to others. It's been proven that close relationships in general boost your immune system and add longevity to your life. In fact, study after study shows that married couples live longer than single people. One study taken from *ABC Health & Wellbeing* compared the death rate of 1,000 married couples to that of 1,000 single people. The death rate doubled in single people from the ages of 70-84 years of age. Now, if you are single, no worries because you don't have to get married to have close relationships.

"It is better living in a tent on a beach with someone you love than a mansion by yourself." Jim Rohn

Jim Rohn said it best. He believed this is one of the keys to living the "good life". I couldn't agree with him more. That's why family is my second cornerstone.

When my wife and I met, it was instant chemistry. Six months after dating, we decided to move in together. It was one of those things where we were best friends. We didn't have much money then, but spending all our time together was priceless. It was rough financially in those days, but I had a wonderful family here in Georgia. The beautiful thing about my family is that we welcomed all people in. There was a lot of love in my family; so, my wife felt very comfortable. All of her family was in Mississippi and California.

My Aunt Pam, who was like a second mom to me, let us rent her in-law suite. She wanted us to stay there so we could save up money for a house. While living there, we had our daughter. I already had a son in Connecticut from a previous relationship who stayed with me during the summer. We had officially outgrown that one bedroom in-law suite. It was time to get our own place. We worked very hard and finally saved enough money to buy our first house. I will never forget how happy my wife was because of our accomplishment. It wasn't the best house looking back at it, but we were excited.

As our family grew, we moved on and purchased a larger home. However, I realized that it was never about the size of the house or even having a house at all for that matter. It was about going through and making it out of the struggle with the one you love. It's about living and sharing those life experiences with the ones you call family. It's about a collective connectedness.

Some people believe that struggle is bad. Let's go back to our first cornerstone for a second, faith. Faith is one of the essential keys to making it through tough times. Remember, we are building a life beyond our imagination.

In order to build, you have to destroy. When a garden is created, you have to destroy the ground by digging and cultivating it for something new to reside there. Sometimes struggle is sent your way to see who is going to be standing with you when it's all over. Anything worth having that is substantial in your life has to be met with adversity. It's the law of opposites or polarity. It simply states everything has its opposite. You can't have hot without cold or good without bad. So when you are building something good in your life, you are most certain to encounter some "bad" things.

Family makes those encounters easier. They allow you not to have to go through those encounters alone. You might say, "I don't have any family." Remember human beings have an innate emotion of belongingness. Family is not always a bloodline. It can be friends, business colleagues or people in the same organization as you. There is a story in the Bible that has always stuck with me in Mathew 12:46 taken from the New International Version:

While Jesus was still talking to the crowd, his mother and brothers stood outside, wanting to speak to him. Someone told him, "Your mother and brothers are standing outside, wanting to speak to you." He replied to him, "Who is my mother, and who are my brothers?" Pointing to his disciples, he said. "Here are my mother and my brothers. For whoever does the will of my Father in heaven is my brother and sister and mother."

So, you see, family can be considered those who believe as you do.

We have all heard the saying "You can't choose your family". There is some truth to that because your parents are your parents. However, you can choose your team. When building the life beyond your imagination, you will need a winning team. I'm not talking about just in business, but in all areas of your life. The team (family) is crucial to your success. **T**ogether **E**veryone **A**chieves **M**ore!

Throughout history we have always done amazing things as a group of people. Today, I see most people trying to become successful all alone. It doesn't happen that way. It's almost like the universe conspires against you. When it is a higher purpose and not driven from the ego or selfishness, then greater success can be achieved.

I want you to take a deeper look. Understand why the principle of family is important. Take a look at yourself for a moment. When you look in the mirror, you see one person. Now let's place you under a huge microscope so we can really see you. When we take the whole person under microscopic view, you now see tiny atoms moving quickly. Those atoms make molecules, which make up cells. Then, your cells form tissues. Tissues form organs and organs are a part of a particular system. The end result is you in the totality. Not to give you a science lesson, but I want you to see that even in the appearance of one, that one is made up of many.

There is something about the cornerstone of family that pushes human beings to excel. It pushes us toward a purpose greater than ourselves. Family is an extension of you. When you ask most mothers or fathers why they go to work every day most of them will say, "So, I can take care of my family". You see, the thought pattern of family is of, for, and by each other. It has existed in us since the beginning. When you hear statements like, "The needs of the many outweigh the needs of a few," you can find some truth to this.

I remember seeing my mother pregnant with her last child in the dead of winter. I'm not sure if you know how winters can be in New England, but they can take a toll on the body. She would get up and catch the city transit to work in the snow. She was taking care of three of us at the time and we were soon to have a fourth addition to the family. We stayed in what we called, "the projects" or low-income housing. We had two bedrooms; so, my sister and I shared a room and my brother stayed in the room with our mother. I was 11 at the time but looking back I can remember my mom being tired a lot. Our father didn't live with us; so, as the oldest, I helped my mother the best I could. As soon as I turned thirteen, I started working to bring in extra money to help my mom and my family.

Scenarios like this are happening all around the world. I'm sure my mother would have loved to take some time off every once in a while. This is a prime example of the needs of many outweighing the needs of a few.

The beautiful thing about the power of creation is that you have access to that same power. If you were born into a family that isn't your idea of what family should be, you can create your own. There are a lot of families out there that are considered dysfunctional. Most of us who are old enough have watched *The Oprah Winfrey Show* at some point in our lives, and we see or hear about the stories: *"My father abused me"* or *"My mother never loved me"* or *"My sibling destroyed my life"*. Twenty years later, that person is stuck psychologically because of what happened in their childhood. How do you overcome that?

How do you move on from that? It's not like you can take those experiences away as if they never existed. It is your past. I know it is traumatic, but that's why they call it history. The only time that exists is right now. Just declare to yourself: "I want help now. I want to get better now." You can be taught how to bury that emotional pain from the past deep and lock it behind a steel door forever. It's the power of visualization and manifestation. We have to learn how to replace that which is bad in our minds with something good.

For example, if your father wasn't in your life growing up, and it hurts you emotionally when you have children, you can be there for your children. Don't repeat the cycle of pain! Don't make excuses about what you didn't have in your life so you don't know any better. That may have been so, but now you know better. You know how it made you feel; so, do not become selfish and continue that cycle. Nothing good comes out of holding on to past pain, I promise.

Create the family environment you know can exist, not only at home, but also in business as well. Hold true to your values and never compromise them for things that are very transient like money or other material things. In essence, all things are transient. We live on through our lineage; so, live for something great. Live for the family you leave behind after you pass on. Live for the ideas you gave birth to that became tangible through hard work and dedication.

The family is one of nature's masterpieces. - George Santayana

THREE

Fitness

"Take care of your body. It's the only place you have to live". – Jim Rohn

This is one of the best quotes I have seen on fitness. Our bodies are so complex. We may never completely understand all of the intricate details of its workings or non-workings for that matter.

Society has changed from the times of old. As we move further into our future, I see fitness moving further away from our families and our educational system. According to www.fitness.gov, today only about 4% of elementary schools, 8% of middle schools, and 2% of high schools offer daily P.E. and only 9 states require recess in elementary schools. President Barack Obama's Presidential Council on

Fitness, Sports & Nutrition "engages, educates, and empowers all Americans to adopt a healthy lifestyle that includes regular physical activity and good nutrition." As part of that initiative, First Lady Michelle Obama has developed the "Let's Move" Campaign to help solve the epidemic of childhood obesity within a generation.

The cornerstone of fitness is very important. Unfortunately, many people neglect fitness. Several years ago, I was working out a client, and I will never forget what he said:

"I have spent the majority of my life building my family and my business so much that I totally neglected my body in the process. When I was young, I spent all my time building my family and acquiring wealth. Now, that I am old I am spending all my money paying you for my health."

We laughed. I have learned a lot from this client on creating a successful business.

Just six years prior to me becoming a professional fitness trainer, I would never forget my own situation. I was never the one to make doctor visits for a routine physical. One day, I felt really strange. It was like I knew there was something wrong with my body. I ignored it and kept going about my daily routine. Running up the stairs was a task for me. I mean I was literally out of breath by the time I got to the top. I was 33 at the time. I remember saying, "I'm too young to be feeling this way." From the shortness of breath, fast heartbeat, and dizziness every once in a while, I knew it was time for a check-up. So, I eventually made an appointment with my doctor just for a routine visit:

After my physical the doctor came in and said, "Mr. Parker, how have you been feeling?"

I said, *"For the most part okay, just some shortness of breath and a little dizzy every now and again.*

He said, *"Well, that's because you have hypertension."*

I knew high blood pressure ran on both sides of my family, but I always thought I was too young to have those issues.

He placed me on 50 milligrams of Lisinopril and a diuretic. I was furious! I thought, *"I'm too young for this! I can't believe I have to take medication in my early thirty's!"*

I was 240 lbs at the time. I soon started project weight loss! My entertainment attorney (and friend), Tanya Mitchell Graham, started me on the path to fitness. She said, *"Hey, I have an extra membership that I am not using. Let's work out together."* I knew I had to make a change if I wanted to live a better quality of life. After six months of eating clean and working out 4 days a week, I did it! I got down to a whopping 190 lbs! And now, almost 10 years later I still weigh on average 190 lbs and maintain my health to the best of my abilities. Come to find out even after getting in the best shape of my life, I still had to regulate my blood pressure with medicine because it was hereditary on both sides. However, instead of taking 50 milligrams of Lisinopril *and* a diuretic, I got down to only taking 10 milligrams of Lisinopril. For what it's worth, I am in "perfect health".

A good fitness foundation is important for the longevity and well-being of us all. We cannot leave our physical fitness up to the schools and presidential campaigns. It has to start at home. My wife and I, along with our children, exercise together as a family. It is important to instill those values in our children at a young age. My oldest son, Kedar, was on the verge of being diabetic

four years ago. Weighing 260 lbs at 6'1"
back then, I decided to get him in the gym.
He had seen my transformation and
wanted to follow in those footsteps. I am
proud to say he is in the best shape of his
life at 19. He keeps his weight between
215-220 lbs. Now at 6'3", he eats
healthier and stays in the gym
consistently. This is one of the situations
where leading by example has paid off.
Many of us are not willing to lead by
example, but rather delegate those
responsibilities to others without having
done the recommended actions ourselves.
We have to be willing to light the torch,
run with it, and then pass it along.

*An object in motion will stay in motion
unless acted upon by an equal or a stronger
force. - Isaac Newton*

Now, I won't go into a whole bunch
of physics for you. Simply put, a body in
motion tends to stay in motion. An active
lifestyle increases our chances of long-
term survival.

Over the past few decades, human beings have been consuming more grains, soy and other processed foods. In fact, around 65-70% of our caloric intake is derived from grains and soy. Technology has allowed us to create food quickly and abundantly through processing. Our bodies were made to function best on whole, unprocessed foods with healthy fats, lean protein, fruits and vegetables. The reason most of us in the western society are overweight or obese is because of our diet. Changing our diet will not only lean our bodies, but will also rid our bodies of things like irritability, depression, diabetes, arthritis, heart disease, and hypertension. We have to remain consistent with our diet in order for things to change. Here is an excerpt out of the New Living Translation Version Bible. Daniel 1:10-15:

But he responded, "I am afraid of my lord the king, who has ordered that you eat this food and wine. If you become pale and thin compared to the other youths your age, I am afraid the king will have me beheaded." Daniel spoke with the attendant who had been appointed by the chief of staff to look after Daniel, Hananiah, Mishael, and Azariah. Please test us for ten days on a diet of vegetables and water," Daniel said. "At the end of the ten days, see how we look compared to the other young men who are eating the king's food. Then make your decision in light of what you see." The attendant agreed to Daniel's suggestion and tested them for ten days. At the end of the ten days, Daniel and his three friends looked healthier and better nourished than the young men who had been eating the food assigned by the king.

I know several people who do fad diets and may lose 10-20 lbs after it's over. A diet for 10 days or even 3 weeks for that matter is not a substitute for healthy eating most of the time. If you diet for 30 days and lose 20 lbs, I promise you will gain it back within the next 335 days in the year. Statistics say that 70 to 90 percent of all people who diet and lose weight will gain all the weight back between 1 and 3 years.

Before I put people on a training program, I tell them it will not work if you don't put 80% into changing your diet. I promise you it's not rocket science. There are a lot of variables, yes. I try to keep it simple for people. We are allotted a certain amount of calories for our body type, weight, height, sex, and daily activities. If you go over those allotted calories, YOU WILL gain weight over time. It takes 3500 calories to either lose or gain a pound.

Hormones and metabolism do play a role in weight loss or gain. Now, I have had many clients use this information to create excuses to not even try. They would say, *I don't think I can lose weight* or *my metabolism doesn't work* or *my hormones are out of wack*. It may be true that biochemical changes are taking place in their body; however, it is no excuse for a bad diet or a poor exercise program. You see when people say things like this, they are destroying the very first cornerstone to make all things possible, faith! Fear becomes the winner for a person who is afraid to try. Remember fear robs you of your faith.

Here's the thing, if you are real serious about your fitness, hire a trainer to hold you accountable. Get an accountability partner like I did. My lawyer and I would hold each other accountable for being at the gym when we said we would be. I mean if a high-powered family and entertainment attorney can take time out to do so, I'm sure you can as well.

It's all about time management, which is a crucial key to your success. One thing we all have in common despite our socio-economic status, our race, or religion, is we have the same twenty-four hours in a day. If there are 168 hours in a week and you spend 56 hours sleeping (assuming you get 8 hours a night), 50 hours a week working (including commute time), 28 hours a week with family or significant other, and 21 hours a week on leisure activities. That still leaves 13 hours for exercise!

According to the American Heart Association, all that is required is 150 minutes per week of moderate exercise or 75 minutes per week of vigorous exercise. The easiest goal to remember is 30 minutes a day 5 days a week. That's less than 3 hours a week and you still have 10 hours left!

If you want better results, you have to become better at challenging yourself, not only in the gym, but also in the kitchen. You see, desire is not enough. "Desire" has to meet its sibling "Discipline". Once discipline kicks in, that will get you closer to your destination! Now you are living in 3D. Desire + Discipline = Destination. If discipline diminishes, it will take you further away from your destination and create a lack of desire.

I have helped many people get physically fit in my business. Unfortunately, there are those that may never be physically fit. This isn't to say that they can't. It's just in their minds they feel they can't. I cannot stress the importance of our first cornerstone enough. You really have to believe it can happen to you. I don't mean after hearing a speech or sermon on motivation and then going back to your old habits. I mean it really has to become a part of your lifestyle.

The mind is very illusive. One thing I have learned how to do, and I teach some of my clients this as well, is what I call mind-training. I consider myself a mind coach. We have to condition our minds for survival. The law of self-preservation is simply the innate desire to stay alive and the instinct for individual preservation. This is not only biological, but also psychological. You have to condition your mind into believing, *"If I don't do this I am going to die"*. Once you truly believe this, motivation will no longer be the deciding factor on your workouts.

Never wait for the right feeling to start something. You must execute first and the feeling will follow. When you did a workout in the past, how many times did you say, *I don't feel like working out today* but once you finished you were glad you did? The feeling came afterwards. That's because there is a chemical in the brain known as endorphins. Endorphins are the brain's neurotransmitters that are released during exercise to naturally reduce stress and pain. Stress and pain are the two common factors for the release of this hormone. That's why working out is so beneficial to relieving stress. My wife loves when I come from the gym after a work out because of how happy I am afterwards.

Many think of fitness as a look. If someone has a small frame they are thought to be "in shape". Shape has nothing to do with fitness. I have trained clients who appear to be "in shape" but their ability to do anything aerobic or anaerobic for that matter wasn't much. Fitness has to be more of a lifestyle for you.

There are three body types that exist: Ectomorphic - someone who is skinny in appearance, Mesomorphic- someone of a muscular frame (who seems to put on muscle just by looking at weights), and Endomorphic - someone larger in appearance with more fat than muscle definition.

No matter which of the three body types you have, you can still become physically fit within your body type. America has created a superficial society that we all at some point buy into. Listen, forget about how it looks, if you are overweight and have certain medical conditions, it is dangerous. Do it for the health benefits. Become the best you and be happy with it. Don't buy into the image of what America has defined as beautiful. Remember, you create the world you desire internally first. Then, I promise you the external world would be much greater than you ever imagined.

Set small realistic goals that you are sure to follow. People always ask me, *"How can I lose 50 lbs in a month or two?"* I ask them, *"Did you gain 50 lbs in a month or two?"* The answer is usually, "no". You see, living in a microwave society has conditioned us to want it **now**. I'm not saying don't set big goals; I'm saying big goals are reached through a process of smaller ones.

You know why New Year's Resolutions fail? Because most people say *I'm going to lose weight this year. I'm going to make more money this year. I'm going to stop smoking this year.* It doesn't happen like that. Everything has a compound effect.

When you approach your goals towards your success one day at a time and evaluate what you have accomplished at week's end, then you will start to change the course of your life. Six months to a year from now following this formula will only lead to your success. Don't plant the seed and dig it up a week or two later because it hasn't grown. Let nature do its work. Let God do His part. Allow the season for -growth to happen. Plant more seeds and soon you will have your garden of success.

Exercise to stimulate, not to annihilate. The world wasn't formed in a day, and neither were we. Set small goals and build upon them. –Lee Haney

FOUR

Finance

"It is well enough that people of the nation do not understand our banking and monetary system, for if they did, I believe there would be a revolution before tomorrow morning."- Henry Ford

When it comes to finance, I have found that most people are afraid to talk about money issues. The mental foundation laid here in the past has to be obliterated. According to The Council For Economic Education, only 17 states require high school students to take a personal finance course in order to graduate. That's alarming considering the state of our economy. If we want more success in our economy, we must educate our youth on how finances work and let them make the choice.

I believe finances shouldn't be that forbidden tattoo that you have hidden underneath your clothes as a teenager in hopes that your parents will never see it. You can't build a strong foundation on things if you are afraid of it or never discuss it. The perpetual cycle of poor finances has invaded and germinated in the poor and middle class communities.

Growing up, my parents never taught me about finances, and that's probably because their parents never truly understood them as well. I make it a part of my family's culture to understand finances and how they work. Even my 9 year old is becoming quite the economist. A lot of people are under the assumption that debt can never be eliminated. If you are the creator of that debt, then you can become the eliminator of that debt.

Let's go into the definition of capitalism. Taken from Merriam-Webster dictionary:

Capitalism: an economic system characterized by private or corporate ownership of capital goods, by investments that are determined by private decision, and by prices, production, and the distribution of goods that are determined mainly by competition in a free market.

"Capitalism" is the word that most people cringe at. I believe it's really just a lack of understanding of what the word really means. It's really not that bad when you understand it. What I am about to go into is never taught in school.

"Son, make sure you save your money for when you become older" is what I kept hearing from my family when I was younger. *"Make sure you get good grades and go to college so you can have a good career",* was another one I heard. While there's nothing wrong with those statements and they sound like good gestures, most people are in for a rude awakening. Here is the scenario for most Americans:

You graduate from high school, get into a good college. You meet someone after college and start dating. You get a "good" job, for some at least. You end up getting married and having children. You buy a home, get two cars and a couple of credit cards and you are living the American Dream.

This is how the system works for most Americans. Now, you are a part of a fading middle class. We are programmed from childhood to live like this. You see, you have to remember how capitalism works. You have to become aware of the "big three": government, banks, and big businesses. Once you know how it all works, then you can kind of override the program that has been taught from childhood. We are programmed from grade school to get a good education, which is great. I believe education is one of the most critical things for the advancement of our human culture.

So, here you are ready for college. You take out several student loans to get in. Now, you have graduated and you are looking for a job in your field. While in school you studied things that you are passionate about, but unfortunately that field doesn't pay a lot. You get the job in your field, and now you are rolling. The pay is not the greatest, but it's in your field of study at least. You get married and have kids. You have a mortgage, car notes, credit cards and your everyday expenses on top of paying off those student loans every month. Now, you are in a dilemma. Your pay is not enough for all of these new liabilities you have. So, what do you do? You take out a loan or maybe a second mortgage so you will have some extra cash. Well, that might seem like the best thing to do except now you are in even deeper debt. No worries. They have this new position at your job, but it requires another degree or more training. You have seen the commercials on television.

"Not making enough money at your job? Tired of that job that doesn't pay you enough to support your family? Well, come to so and so college so you can have the career of your dreams."

"That's it!" you reply. Now, you are back in school.

Understand how it all works. The "big three" are structured to work simultaneously. Nearly 20 million Americans attend college each year and of that 20 million, 12 million borrow annually to help cover cost (Taken from *Chronicles of Higher Education*). The banks provide student loans. The government guarantees the banks that you will repay these loans. You now go work for the big businesses so you can pay off your debt. In this process, choosing to earn income through a job allows taxes to eat away at your finances.

As an employee, you are taxed anywhere from 28-33% of your pay. So, if you make $50,000 a year, you might bring home $34,000 after taxes. Now, you have other expenses like your mortgage, student loans, car notes, and credit cards each month. You pay the banks' interest when you acquire these types of expenses. Big businesses (utility companies, supermarkets, etc...) are responsible for taking the remainder of your paycheck. You now have to pay utilities, buy clothing, food, and don't forget other luxuries you may want to purchase. There is nothing wrong with nice things; it's just that most middle class and poor Americans spend money on luxuries *first*.

This is the cycle. You see, out of this process the American Dream becomes a nightmare. A financial tsunami is in the making. This is the pattern that is becoming more prevalent in this country. The problem is that most Americans are not even aware it is even happening. Most consider this to be "normal" living. In capitalism, if you are not careful, you can spend your whole life drowning in this financial tsunami.

The problem is inflation, taxes, debt, and just poor financial decision-making. When food, gas and other expenses go up, it's as if your pay goes down. Your dollar is no longer the same due to inflation. When gas goes up, trucking companies who deliver food from farmers to grocery stores raise their prices. In return, farmers and grocery stores raise their prices so you are stuck paying more for the same goods. Your job does not compensate you when this happens.

Taxes are another nightmare for most Americans. The more money you make in your job, the higher the tax bracket. From the earlier example, if you are trying to live off of a $50,000 a year salary, it's really only $34,000. You have to compensate for the government's share. The problem here is most Americans aren't aware of tax laws. Tax evasion is never a solution to tax problems. Tax protection is a much better option.

Being an employee puts you in a higher tax bracket. Business owners end up paying less taxes overall because of the tax laws given to businesses. Businesses are awarded more deductions than someone earning their income from being an employee. So, instead of paying 24-33% of your income in taxes, as a business owner, that number is reduced to 18-23% due to tax benefits. This becomes the difference of thousands to millions of dollars depending on your financial scenario.

I never understood taxes and how they worked in the favor of businesses until my attorney and friend, Tanya Mitchell Graham, introduced me to the process. Although, I had an entrepreneurial spirit at a young age, I still was "new" to how the process really worked. We were part owners of an entertainment company. While traveling with our artists, she would save every single receipt. She said to me, *"This is a part of our tax deductions as business owners. We get a portion of our meals, entertainment and travel to write off as business expenses."* While in law school, she told me that all of her electives were in tax law.

When given the option of owning your own business or being an employee, most people choose the latter. While there's nothing wrong with being an employee, you will find more financially successful people are business owners and investors. The taxes alone are a great benefit. Out of the three income choices (earned income, business income, and investment income), investment income is the most lucrative for tax benefits. Capital gain (profits made from investments) taxes will be about 15%, which is much lower than the tax on individual income earned as an employee. Capital gains would be your best scenario for earning your income.

Take someone who may earn one million dollars with earned income and someone who has earned one million dollars from their investment or capital gains. Let's look at the tax differences. Someone earning one million dollars in earned income as an employee (W-2) may pay $350,000 in taxes while someone who has capital gains of one million dollars may pay $150,000 in taxes. That is a difference of $200,000!

I teach people with earned income to start a part-time business where they can earn some extra cash and get all the tax benefits of being a business owner. By doing so, they are now restructuring their financial future. They are now turning things around in their favor. They are now creating that American Dream you always heard about.

Now take that extra money and pay off some debt, which in return creates more of a positive cash flow. You know those credit cards that were at 21% APR? Pay those off. Guess what? You have now returned 21% of someone else's interest back into your household. Now, that's a great 21% return you can use to build upon your dreams. It's simple; your money is going to make someone wealthy, so it might as well be you!

Most people are afraid of that "B" word. Starting your own business is not that difficult nowadays. In fact, you don't have to go as far as spending a lot of capital you don't have. Opening a food franchise can cost anywhere from 200 thousand to 2 million dollars, depending on the name.

We are in a new day and age because of media and technology. In fact, the benefits of home-based business are becoming more and more practical for most Americans. You can start a home-based business for as little of $200 to $2000 with a one-time investment. There are hundreds of companies out there.

You just have to find the right one for you. Turn the things you like to do such as your hobbies, or things you're good at into a home-based business. You can market and sell your goods or services right out of the comfort of your home with products ranging from beauty supplies, health and fitness, to a broad array of other products and services.

The benefits of owning a home-based business is that you now have the same tax write-offs of someone who owns 10 McDonalds! A portion of your utilities, square footage for your home, meals, travel and much more are now tax-deductible.

Why is this cornerstone so important along with the other three? The proper finances allow you more freedom. The key is to not fight against capitalism, but understand how it works, and make it work best for you and your family. It's the lack of understanding that causes us to suffer from what we don't know. The best investment we will ever have in life is in one's self. That's why I don't knock education. College is great; just understand how the financial process works in its completion. Don't get pushed into the tsunami.

What is the purpose of an investment? To put it in simple terms, an investment is an asset or item that is purchased with the hope that it will generate income in the future. Okay, great! Well, why do investments exist in capitalism? I don't want to bore you with a lot of economic and financial jargon. Let's keep it simple. Here is an example:

A person has an idea of a product or service they want to take to the marketplace. They lack the necessary resources to bring it completely to fruition. They use whatever capital they have to start, but they will need assistance from others to really get things going. An investor is needed to grow this idea for this product or service to come to the marketplace. As the creator of this idea, you are willing to pay a certain percentage of your capital back to the investor for the use of their financial resources. If the idea is a success, then your business grows and the investor gets a certain return on their initial investment into your idea.

In the financial world, there is a rule called the Rule of 72. The Rule of 72 states that in order to find the number of years required to double your money at a given interest rate, you divide the compound return into 72. *For example, if you want to know how long it would take to double your money at 12% interest, divide 12 into 72 and you get 6 years.*

The problem most people have is they aren't aware that just working hard and saving your money actually does more damage than good. In the grand scheme of things, when you are looking at building wealth, it's based on more strategic things instead of a "roll of the dice." There are no guarantees in life; there is only guidance.

You see putting your money in a savings account that only gives you 1-2% return will be counterproductive for growth if inflation is at 4% or higher. This is what happens:

A bottle of Coke 50 years ago in 1964 cost 15 cents. Today, you will pay $1 to $3 for it. Let's say you pay $1 today. Let's put a dollar into your savings account back then earning 2% interest. Today, you would have $2.72. Let's look at inflation for a moment and your savings earning potential from the bank. Before inflation if you take that $2.72 you earned you could buy 18 bottles of Coke. After 50 years with inflation you can now only buy 2 Cokes!

Saving at that rate will never outpace inflation. This is one of the reasons most Americans at the age of 65 have to go back to work. The cost of living has increased dramatically. So, the money that you had 40 to 50 years ago is not the same money today. You now need double the amount to survive.

There are solutions to these financial challenges. What changed for me is first having the faith that I could change my financial situation. The next thing was finding the right information. So, I started my search reading any and every book by people I thought were successful. This was my new focus in life. Remember, what you focus on is what you will attract to you. I started meeting some very successful business people, Marquel Russell, Brian Beane, and Ivey Stokes. These three gentlemen further advanced my quest on financial education.

Marquel Russell's company, Infinite Success University, has a successful business coaching and training program that helps many people in personal growth and self-development.

Brian Beane, who retired from corporate America at age 22 and made his first million dollars from home in his twenties has a company called Mentor to Millions. He has trained on stages in front of thousands of people and has stood alongside people such as Les Brown, Lisa Nichols, and so many others.

Then, there is Ivey Stokes, who has a background in the financial services industry. He has earned 9 figures in business and investments. He is the co-founder of My Econ, a personal financial success company that educates and informs individuals on financial strategies to achieve success.

To be successful in building this cornerstone, you just have to start. Robert Kiyosaki talks about the 3 E's in his book *A Guide To Investing*. Education along with the experience of investing leads to excessive cash. Get started today and live life more abundantly.

Money is not an evil thing, as most would tell you. It's a tool, and everyone knows you can either use the tool for good or for evil. The choice lies within the person.   Timothy 6:10 in The New International Version Bible states:

For the love of money is a root of all kinds of evil. Some people, eager for money, have wandered from the faith and pierced themselves with many grieves.

All that is required to build wealth is wisdom. Once you acquire the knowledge needed and you apply that knowledge, you are well on your way to financial independence. You will no longer get 1 to 2% return on your money. You will get 8-20% return on your money and even more! You will have your money working for you so you can enjoy more of life's treasures that cost nothing at all but time. Out of the two equities of time and money, time is the most valuable. With the right plans in motion, you can be well on your way to financial freedom.

FIVE

Putting It All Together

All of the cornerstones are strong by themselves, but when put together they become a force to be reckoned with. It's like baking a cake. The main ingredients in a cake are flour, butter, milk, eggs and sugar.

Let's take flour for example. Flour makes up the bulk of the cake just like faith makes up the bulk of your success. Don't get me wrong: we all know there are a lot of other things involved in order to succeed. But let's face it; you are not going to pursue something you don't believe in. That's why faith is the key ingredient.

Flour is a powdery substance derived from grinding and mashing the whole grain of wheat. The process alone sounds intensive. Well, so is the process of faith. That same process of grinding and mashing has to be applied to the doubts that enter your mind, the naysayers speaking against you, and all of the things that didn't happen right in your life until this very moment.

Then, you have butter. Most are unaware of the healthy benefits of real butter. Butter is rich in fat-soluble vitamins such as A, E and K2. Vitamin K2 is rare in our modern diet. The health benefits of this vitamin help with calcium metabolism. Low intake of this vitamin is associated with cancer, osteoporosis, and cardiovascular disease. Real butter is also rich in healthy saturated fats, which help raise the "good cholesterol" in the body.

Family is so important today. In it are those rare essentials like vitamin K2 found in real butter. A lack of it can eat away your success like cancer. The very bones of your success will start to degenerate and the heart will be filled with trouble.

Milk and eggs are our next ingredients. They provide three major substances to a cake: water, protein and fat. Without these ingredients, there would be no structure. Just like these ingredients provide structure and "keep it all together", the same is for the cornerstone of fitness.

Fitness is like the eggs and milk in a cake. It provides the proper structure for keeping the body and mind together. It is responsible for the prevention of serious health conditions in the body. Without fitness, you will soon see what you are trying to build slowly deteriorate.

The last ingredient, which is equally as important although some health junkies may not think so, is sugar. Without sugar, our bodies would cease to function properly. Naturally occurring sugars, such as those found in fruit (fructose) and milk (lactose) are beneficial to your diet. Your body converts fructose into glucose. Glucose is the sugar your body metabolizes for energy.

Finances are like the sugar or the "sweet spot" as I like to call it. Like sugar gives the body energy when metabolized, finances do the same thing for our lives. Our bodies can't move without energy. Money allows us to move about freely in a capitalistic society. Having good finances is like a feeling of euphoria. It's kind of like eating that piece of cake with just the right amount of sugar in it.

In order to truly live a life beyond your imagination, you must apply and mix all these areas together to get to the cake. Although each area alone stands strong in their own right, putting all of them together is where all the magic happens. It's where you take things that are good and turn them into something magnificent!

You don't have to focus on all of them at the same time. Focus on the ones you need the most. Remember it's always a process. Things don't "just happen," it's a combination of universal laws that takes place. There are certain causes in life that lead to effects. There is nothing above this law. Although it may look this way in appearance, we all know from the unseen to the seen that there is correspondence.

We must focus and master each cornerstone throughout our lives to obtain true mastery. It's about being whole and complete. I see it all the time, and I analyze my life as well. Far too many times I see people who are strong in faith and family, but lack fitness and finance. I hear things like *"all you need is family"* or *"all you have to have is faith."* I'm not saying there is anything wrong with that, but remember we are talking about it all. *"No one can have it all"*, you say. I beg to differ. It's a matter of your view of *"it all"*. Now, we all know if you are talking about the literal sense of "all things" and having possession of them, then no. I am referring to all the things that truly matter like these 4 areas of your life.

Then, there are those I see having their finances and faith in order, but have no principles of family and fitness incorporated in their lives. I have met many financially successful people whose health is slowly fading because of neglect. I have even heard them go as far as saying *"I don't need family"* and *"Who needs fitness, I have money"*. They hide behind a false cloak of insecurities with their money. Their faith only resides in getting more finances for selfish gains.

We must put it all together in order to be complete. There is a season for it all. Don't settle for just being balanced in a couple of these cornerstones. Be willing to go beyond your imagination and push pass those mental limitations you have put on your life. Be willing to work on those areas that you are weak in. You don't have to go at it alone. Remember the win of the championship is a shared success. Get people to help you who are strong in the areas where you are weak.

If you lack strong faith, dedicate time around someone who is an expert in the field of faith. If you are weak in the area of family, get with experts who can teach you and instill in you what you would like your definition of family to be. In the area of fitness, hire a personal trainer or nutritionist to help you properly nourish and train your body. If your finances are in disarray, hire a financial advisor.

There are many things that are needed to be complete. I'm not going into the small details. I want you to look at it like the cake. These are the four areas of your life that when all put together will be the most amazing experience. Of course, there will always be higher levels in each of the areas that you can go to. There will always be ebbs and flows in all things.

Just know that when all these cornerstones are put together in your life, you will become the creator of a life beyond your imagination.

SIX

Foundation

I've come to believe that all my past failure and frustrations were actually laying the foundation for the understandings that have created the new level of living I now enjoy. –Tony Robbins

Foundation is most important for building anything that will last throughout the times. When building in these areas of your life, you have to start with the very first tool, your mind. Before things become physical they are created on the mental plane. This is why it's so important to control your thoughts. Over time, the focus of a person's thinking will ultimately create and shape what they know to be life.

The mind is the connection between the physical world and emotional world.

In fact, in many studies they have found how the mind can alter physical conditions of disease found in the body. Best-selling author, Dr. Lissa Rankin, speaks about this in her book entitled, *Mind Over Medicine*. She has conducted extensive scientific research and case studies on what the medical world calls *spontaneous remission*. Spontaneous remission is an unexpected improvement or cure from a disease that appears to be progressing in its severity. She teaches her patients something she calls *the six steps to healing yourself*. The first step is belief. This isn't a coincidence. You see, no matter what area of your life you are trying to improve, you will need the first cornerstone of faith in order to accomplish it.

What are you building your foundation on? When building the foundation, you have to choose very carefully. Structures built on crystalline bedrock can support up to 12,000 pounds per square foot of load-bearing pressure.

Building on fine-grained soils like clay and silt are not good because they absorb water, which leads to shifts and cracks in the foundation.

Your mind, which is the foundation of building the 4 cornerstones to your success, must be built of solid rock. When troubled waters come, you will be prepared. When strong winds, come you will be protected. Taking the easy way out is a sure way to complete disaster. Sure, you may have the appearance of success on the outside. Many onlookers will marvel at the life you have built, not knowing that as soon as the winds of life blow, in it will crumble. Those who build on shaky ground will never sustain a structure strong enough to stand the tests of life. They will be buried in their own ruins. Taking shortcuts for the appearance of victory is nothing but an eventual forfeit.

I hear many people say that they just want *a quick fix, a magic pill, something that will get me immediate results.* Our society is so fixated with speed. Just look in your automobile for instance. We have laws that say the speed limit is anywhere from 55 to 70 mph on some interstates. However, the automobile industry makes vehicles that go anywhere from 120 to 270 mph!

There is a phrase in the urban community that states, "Don't fall for the *okie-doke*", meaning don't fall for the scam or don't believe in the lie. I am here to tell you the same. You hear so many things like, *"Do this and you will have amazing results in just 7 days."* Or one of my favorites, *"You can fire your boss! Create instant financial success in just 30 days!"* While there are some dramatic cases where a person goes through extreme measures and discipline and achieves success in a short period of time; however, that is not the norm. Besides, it is nearly impossible to perform at those levels for long periods of time before burnout sets in. You will find out that success is a steady progression of consistent actions done over the course of time. Besides this, expeditious mentality only leads to the depletion of faith when situations go wrong. You must learn patience and practice the art of delayed gratification.

Failure is expected throughout life, that's why the importance of a solid foundation is a must. There is a difference when failure falls upon solid structure. Many people who are extremely successful in things have failed hundreds, if not thousands, of times. Henry Ford failed and went broke 5 times before he succeeded. His company is now the oldest automobile company in America. I believe Zig Ziglar said it best in cases like this, *"Remember that failure is an event, not a person."* The mind will perceive events as good or bad. Events and circumstances that have gone bad or not according to intention should be viewed as learning lessons. Circumstances of such are merely stepping-stones to greater heights for the person whose mind is made up.

Conclusion

The cards are in your favor! Even if you were born into poverty, suffer from physical conditions that limit your mobility, abandoned in your childhood, and have lost all of your faith, the cards are in your favor. The only thing that is consistent is change. You can change! You say that's absurd. You might think, "I can't bounce back from all those setbacks. Someone like me never makes it out." Yes, someone like you *can* bounce back; someone like you *can* build a life beyond imagination. Someone like you has made it out! You have to decide if that next someone will be you. *YOU* write the story to your life; no one else! The cards are in your favor!

You say life isn't fair. Well, is it supposed to be? I mean when you look at the definition of life never does it include "being fair" in the definition. Life is the condition that distinguishes animals and plants from inorganic matter including the ability to reproduce, grow and carry on functional activity until death. In one word, let's sum it all up into what we call "existence". How you exist is based on the mental foundation you lay. This is the first tool to building your monolithic edifice!

You have more power than you think. The mind can be your best friend or worst enemy. The battlefield resides there. Creation exists there first, and then it becomes physical. Things happen twice, first in the mind, and then in the physical; so make sure you handle the first step and all else will follow. If life dealt you a bad hand, learn how to stack the deck. Add the cards you want in your life. Only you have the power to do so. You can draw from the ever-abundant deck that God and the universe has provided for you, or you can believe there aren't any more cards left.

You have to make it work in your favor because no one else can play your hand.

Look at your life up until now. Which of the 4 cornerstones needs building upon? Which one is most important to you to build next? You can't build them all at once. The building of great structure is laid one brick at a time. Concentrate on that one area and build from there. There is a wonderful place waiting for you at your completion. If and only if you start now, you can move from imagination of that life you dreamed of to living it. Let's Go!

Visit www.visualizedwealth.com further information on the author and company. This book was put together to help people know the importance of these four areas in their lives. Through personal experience, challenges and education, author Dre Parker has revealed to you the 4 secret areas that will be the difference in creating a life beyond imagination. Visualized Wealth was created to inform, educate and help individuals create a life in wealth, not just financial, but in all areas of life. True wealth (well-being) is the completion and mastery of all 4 cornerstones. Not only is giving back essential to the continued growth of our existence as human beings, but it also causes circulation in the universe. Two things are happening in the universe and that's either congestion or circulation. Either you are contributing to the flow (circulation) of things or you are causing things to stop (congestion). We choose to be a part of the circulation and donate $1 for each book sold to help fight against lung cancer, in memory of Pamela Joi Jones-Ashbourne, Carolyn "Dinkey" Lockhart, and Thelma Holley.

Please visit:
www.visualizedwealth.com

87

WWW.VISUALIZEDWEALTH.COM

OUR MISSION

Visualized Wealth Marketing LLC was started for the sole purpose of creating more value in individuals. Our mission statement is simple: "Creating Value in Others For A Life Envisioned in Wealth."

THE 4 CORNERSTONES

We help individuals build in what we believe are the four most important areas of one's life. Faith, family, fitness, finance are the key components that help build a life beyond imagination.

FOUNDATION

In our personal and business consulting services the very first thing we teach is foundation. The first tool required to build a solid foundation in your personal, as well as business life, is your mind. Our CEO Dre Parker uses the term "mind coach" for what we consider the most influential part of your success.

I AM SUCCESS

The Visualized Wealth Marketing "I Am Success" campaign was designed to promote awareness of what success truly is. We educate our youth on how success is more of an idea that is pursued and seen to completion rather than social economic status.

SHOP OUR ONLINE STORE FOR A
VARIETY OF EDUCATIONAL AND
INSPIRATIONAL ITEMS FROM BOOKS TO
T-SHIRTS TO DVDS.

OUR SERVICES

USE OUR SERVICES TO FIT YOUR PERSONAL OR BUSINESS NEEDS FROM GRAPHIC & WEB DESIGN, T-SHIRT PRINTING, AUDIO & VIDEO RECORDING AND EDITING, PERSONAL FITNESS TRAINING, PERSONAL GROWTH & SELF DEVELOPMENT, AND PERSONAL FINANCIAL SOLUTIONS.

WWW.VISUALIZEDWEALTH.COM

www.ingramcontent.com/pod-product-compliance
Lightning Source LLC
Chambersburg PA
CBHW070107070426
42448CB00038B/2026